SUMMARY

&ANALYSIS

OF

GAME
CHANGERS

What Leaders, Innovators, and Mavericks Do to Win at Life

A GUIDE TO THE BOOK
BY DAVE ASPREY

NOTE: This book is a summary and analysis and is meant as a companion to, not a replacement for, the original book.

Please follow this link to purchase a copy of the original book: https://amzn.to/2UEh6UT

TABLE OF CONTENTS

SYNOPSIS

For five years, Dave Asprey, the *New York Times* bestselling author of books like *Head Strong* and *The Bulletproof Diet* and "professional biohacker," had one-on-one conversations with 450 unusually impactful people from different fields—scientists, athletes, innovative MDs, Navy SEALs, personal development leaders, shamans, and monks—about their secrets to performing better and statistically analyzed their replies. It began with his extremely popular podcast *Bulletproof Radio*, which, in turn, was a result of his nineteen-year multimillion-dollar personal crusade to upgrade himself.

Their cumulative wisdom and Asprey's own research has helped him lose weight, improve his IQ, sleep better, and have a more successful career and better relationships.

The question he put to each of these game changers was: "If someone came to you tomorrow wanting to perform better as a human being, what are the three most important pieces of advice you'd offer, based on your own life experience?" The patterns that emerged from the data collected from hundreds of interviews reveal a road map involving 46 laws that can offer the reader a better chance at success and happiness.

Most of the advice falls into three broad categories: things that make you smarter, faster, and happier. "Smarter" helps your brain reach peak performance. "Faster" helps tap your mental energy to make your body more efficient. Once you gain some control over your mind and body, you can be "happier."

No one mentioned money, power, or attractiveness—the three definitions of success representing the bacteria-like behavior (fear, feed, procreation) of the mitochondria in our body that essentially govern our consciousness. Game changers don't focus on these primitive mitochondria-driven goals, but manage the energy coming from these organelles to achieve happiness, fulfillment, and success.

PART 1: SMARTER

While there are a number of ways to increase the brain's energy supply and maximize productivity, the easiest way is to stop wasting this energy on things that make you weak.

Law 1: Learn to say No

Master the art of doing things that really matter and create energy, passion, and quality of life. Stewart Friedman, the creator of the Total Leadership Program, recommends imagining yourself twenty years from now to figure out what and who matters to you. Once you have a compelling image of an achievable future, it will serve as a window into your true values and make it easy to decide where to invest your energy.

One way to do this is to set a decision budget. To stay on budget, keep your decision-making limited to tasks that can potentially change the outcome of your overall mission. Making decisions uses up one's willpower, which is like a muscle that gets fatigued with overuse. Decision fatigue sets in your life when you focus on trivial decisions like what to eat and what to wear. Leaders like Mark Zuckerberg and Steve Jobs have realized this, saving time by sticking to a single wardrobe item every day. The "willpower muscle" can be strengthened by successfully doing things you don't want to do, but pushing it beyond its limit doesn't help you.

Law 2: Do not be passive about discovering yourself

Instead of discovering who you are, you become powerful when you decide who you are. Two barriers to achieving personal freedom are: self-oppression (your tendency to put yourself down) and social oppression (people judging you and being unsupportive). You can overcome these barriers through the "competence-confidence-loop." The more you understand a subject, the more confident you get. To be intentional about your aspirations rather than focusing on what is merely practically achievable, record three words (like engaged, grateful, energized, warm, loving, devoted, etc.) that describe your highest, best self and set an alarm to go off three times a day to remind yourself of this aspirational sense of self.

Choose a career that you truly care about. Play to your strengths, and mastery would develop organically.

Prioritize actions into three buckets: things that drain energy, things you don't mind and are important and useful, and things that give you energy and joy and can be called *primal inclinations*. Break your daily actions down so that you spend none of your time on tasks that fall into the first category, 10 percent of your time on the second category, and 90 percent of your time in the final category.

Law 3: Don't just "try"

The words you choose matter a lot, both to other people as well as to your own nervous system. Asprey gives an example from the life of JJ Virgin, a well-known health and wellness expert. Virgin's teenage son was able to recover from a serious road accident because of her insistence on using positive words around the boy, even when he was in coma, so that he understood that recovery was the only option available to him.

Asprey believes in the power of language to drive success. He keeps a list of "weasel words" (Can't, Need, Bad, and Try) that allow speakers to avoid responsibility and give them an excuse to fail.

The recently understood concept of neuroplasticity shows that the brain can grow new cells and forge new neural connections to become smarter, develop new habits, and remember better throughout your life.

According to many of Asprey's guests, good habits are the third most important factor in improving performance, even ahead of education.

Law 4: Question your assumptions

The meditation teacher and founder of Mindvalley, Vishen Lakhiani talks about how his false beliefs about himself, his appearance, and his abilities were shaped by his peers while he was growing up. False beliefs can be overcome by *consciousness engineering*.

Step 1: Recognize your beliefs are just the hardware installed in you long ago that can be upgraded. Modalities like hypnotherapy or meditation can then lead to awakening moments that make you conscious of your beliefs so that you begin to change them intentionally.

When Asprey meditates, he tells his nervous system the universe has his back and that there's a conspiracy to help him succeed. This may not be true, but the positive beliefs make the brain believe them and act on them.

Step 2: Upgrade your system by studying the greats and finding out habits that made a difference for the most impactful people.

Identify moments when you can prevent an automatic response and, instead, guide yourself in a better direction. For example, when someone says something that bothers you, instead of reacting with anger as you normally would (downwiring), pause to consider why the comment upset you so much and then choose with intention how you want to respond (upwiring).

Law 5: Intelligence is about upgrading how you learn

Performing working memory tasks (like the Dual-n-Back test) increases not only your working memory but also all kinds of other fluid intelligence-based skills, from reading comprehension to math ability.

Jim Kwik, the world expert in speed-reading, overcame learning disabilities to master the art of reading with focus by using the F-A-S-T method of reading:

F: Forget

- Temporarily forget what you already know about a subject so you can learn something new.
- Forget your self-limiting beliefs about how smart you are.
- Forget everything that's going around you and focus on what you are reading.

A: Active

- Just as dramatically increasing the weight you lift if you visit the gym infrequently can have the same effect as lifting five-pound weights, intense learning can give you results in less time.
- Take notes actively and share what you learn.
- Take notes the old-fashioned way, with pen and paper. Capture notes on the left side of the page; create notes, i.e., write down your own impressions, on the right.

S: State

- Instead of letting the environment decide your mood, set a high standard for yourself and modify the environment to meet that setting.

T: Teach

- Learn anything as if you have to teach it to others—retention will automatically be better.

Law 6: Learn using images

Teach your brain to think in images rather than words. Learning through visualization comes only next to learning through doing or teaching, but even in the latter process, you engage your visual senses.

The world-changers interviewed by Asprey have rated self-awareness—an intimate understanding of the normally subconscious factors that motivate you and making them conscious—the sixth most important thing for performing better.

Though his guests didn't explicitly say so, Asprey gathered from behind-the-scenes conversations that many of them had tried mind-altering substances like "smart drugs" and nootropics.

The use of mind-enhancing drugs is no different than drinking caffeine to stay awake or popping a Tylenol to get rid of a headache. However, the use of drugs—a part of biohacking—has to be accompanied with other methods like meditation.

Law 7: The use of smart drugs will become more acceptable

LSD, which is taken by high performers like Silicon Valley tech employees and endurance athletes in tiny doses—one-twentieth to one-tenth of a full dose—can lead to increased creativity, positivity, focus, and empathy without the notorious psychedelic effects. It can also increase the production of brain-derived neurotrophic factor (BDNF), a powerful protein that stimulates production of brain cells and strengthens existing ones.

The nootropics Asprey talks about having had the most success with are:

Racetams – Aniracetam is fast acting, reduces stress, and increases your ability to get things into and out of your memory. Phenylpiracetam is highly energizing and stimulating, and is known to benefit patients of stroke, brain damage, and epilepsy. The side effects are minor.

Modafinil (Provigil) – Modafinil improves fatigue levels, motivation, reaction time, and vigilance, and reduces impulsive decision-making. It is not a stimulant but a eugeroic—a wakefulness-promoting agent. Some people develop headaches when using it, and about five in a million can develop a life-threatening autoimmune condition.

Nicotine – Nicotine, without the toxins and carcinogens wrapped around it, gives faster, more precise motor function, sharpens short-term memory, and speeds up reaction time. It shouldn't be used regularly, though, because of high addiction potential and because it dulls the pleasure pathway.

Caffeine – Caffeine is an energy booster, cognitive enhancer, and lowers the risk of developing Alzheimer's disease.

All cognitive enhancers carry some risks; it depends on you whether those risks are worth the rewards. If deciding to experiment with nootropics or smart drugs, be safe, know the local laws, and use medical guidance.

"[Smart drugs] won't make you an enlightened, loving human overnight. If you're an asshole generally, you'll be a bigger one on smart drugs. But the experience of taking these drugs can help you to see your asshole tendencies when you would ordinarily be blind to them." (Asprey, Dave, Kindle Locations 1133-1134).

Law 8: Experiment with altered states

Get out of your own head and access altered states to face your inner demons. Game changers have tried different methods like full-dose psychedelics, sticking EEG electrodes on their heads, advanced breathing exercises—all in the presence of experts, of course.

Ayahuasca has been used by shamans in the Amazon for thousands of years. It contains DMT (dimethyltryptamine), one of the most powerful psychoactive substances on the planet. Apart from a spiritual experience, ayahuasca is also known to significantly decrease depressive symptoms.

Psychedelics are not a panacea, though, and do not work for everyone. Others can try Vipassana or fasting for days. The key is to reach an altered state where you can see your own programming to give you the power to "rewrite your own code." (Asprey, Dave, Kindle Locations 1296-1297).

Law 9: Breathing is the most powerful vital force

Dr. Stanislav Grof, the pioneer of psychedelic research, began searching for alternate tools with the same potential of healing as LSD after the drug was made illegal in the US. He found it in breathing and developed a technique called holotropic breathing, which helps people experience something akin to a psychedelic state.

Many cultures have known of the benefits of breath control for ages. Yogis have practiced pranayama, which is the foundation of the Art of Living breathing techniques.

Law 10: Do not fear failure

You must be fearless. Everyone, including game changers, experience fear, but top performers prevent their bodies from hijacking their creativity and go ahead anyway.

Ravé Mehta, an engineer, professor, award-winning pianist and composer, and founder of Helios Entertainment, discovered that all negative emotions are rooted in fear. Love is the one life force that binds everything together; fear restricts your ability to access love, while trust enables you. Instead of constantly inoculating yourself from getting hurt by blocking your feelings, become vulnerable in the trust that you will not get hurt.

Mehta breaks fear down into three pillars:

- **Time** – Fear is based on what *might* happen in the future. If you are present and receptive in the moment, you are fully trusting.

- **Attachments** – Attachments aren't bad on their own, but they should be gravitational and flexible instead of being rigid, letting you be more confident in your connection with other people and things.

- **Expectation** – Don't expect a specific outcome; have preferences, leaving the door open for different outcomes. You won't feel disappointment, anger, or guilt.

Fear also affects you at your cellular level. One way to overcome this is "rejection therapy," in which you deliberately put yourself in situations where you will face rejection. This celebrates failure and removes one of the greatest fears most people suffer from.

Law 11: Resist being average

When innovating, you will face criticism. Manage your emotional response to these critics and you will forge ahead. Asprey lists a number of medical breakthroughs that wouldn't have been possible had the innovators given up in the face of doubt and criticism.

"...offering gratitude to the people who challenge you is part of overcoming fear." (Asprey, Dave, Kindle Locations 1658-1659).

Law 12: There's no happiness without passion and purpose

Remaining intellectually curious is one of the most important things you can do. To find what you are obsessed about, imagine having everything you want in life. The things you would still want to pursue are what you should be doing now. Making money can't be your goal; it is the by-product of pursuing things you care passionately about making a difference in.

The goal of any education system should be to make children intellectually curious so that they enter the workplace passionate about making a difference. There are four attributes that make up a caring mind-set: straightforward, thoughtful, accountable, and results-driven.

Law 13: Become a professional recovery artist

Contrary to society's teaching of pushing yourself to exhaustion, game changers believe in the importance of downtime.

Pushing yourself to the limit all the time makes your body shut down systems it considers less necessary—systems that keep you young and happy. Stress is the number one factor that triggers the development of symptoms of Hashimoto's disease, a condition in which the immune system attacks the thyroid.

Remove anything from your life that causes stress—inadequate sleep, unhealthy relationships, anger, nutrition deprivation. Practice mindfulness exercises to pause before reacting. Maximize things that give you pleasure.

Upgrade your definition of prosperity, which is typically tied to financial success. Figure out the things most important to you and write down your thirty-, sixty-, and ninety-day goals. Weigh requests for your time against these goals. Small changes, called microhabits, can help change your carelessness with time. Use the Pomodoro Technique—setting a timer for twenty-five minutes to tackle a specific task and then taking a five-minute break to reset.

Law 14: Put yourself first in the morning

The key to creating miracles is putting yourself into the best possible mental, physical, and emotional state possible. Follow the Five-Minute Rule, giving yourself just five minutes to be negative and then stopping the wastage of energy on things you can't change.

Getting into the right state is the most important in the morning, no matter what time you wake up, as it affects the rest of your day. Elrod spends an hour each morning on himself, mainly on meditations and positive visualizations.

PART 2: FASTER

Law 15: Put sexual energy to better use

The game changers didn't mention sex as something needed to succeed, but the topic did come up in many conversations. Sex is one of the three most basic motivations of the human body (apart from fight/flee and feed), so mastering it and being able to redirect the energy into something useful is important.

The act of consciously transforming sexual or any other urge into creativity or physical action is called sublimation. Napoleon Hill, the author of *Think and Grow Rich*, claims that a man's sex drive is the most powerful force he possesses.

According to John Gray, the author of *Men Are from Mars, Women Are from Venus*, paying more attention to hormone imbalances between men and women can improve sex lives and relationships. He recommends having sex once a week to optimize hormone levels. When a monogamous man has sex with a new partner his testosterone level increases. Using Gray's techniques to intentionally keep testosterone levels high can keep you from being tempted to stray.

Chinese Taoists—the world's original biohackers—have recommended transforming sexual energy into immortality. They even had a formula for how often men should ejaculate to maintain youthfulness: (Your age − 7)/4.

Asprey details how following these principles improved his perceived quality of life tremendously.

Law 16: For women, regular orgasms unlock new levels of happiness

In women, orgasms lead to a rise in the levels of hormones related to happiness and performance, improve the immune system, and flood the body with oxytocin, the "love molecule" that fosters bonding, trust, relaxation, and generosity. Dr. Emily Morse, host of the podcast *Sex with Emily*, recommends non-medical ways to boost female libido, like CBD-infused clitoral massage oils and Kegel exercises.

Law 17: Be creative with sex

Orgasms may have different effects on men and women, but there's a spiritual, deeper side to sex, too, where you reach altered states and your body and mind can do more than you think.

Sex often becomes repetitive and less rewarding with time. Setting the climax as the goal also makes you miss out on the entire experience. If one of the partners doesn't reach this goal, there's shame and performance anxiety involved. Remove goals and go off script to truly connect with your partner. Sexual fulfillment can be therapeutic.

Law 18: Porn is the corn syrup of sex

Conscious sex with the right people releases feel-good hormones and neurotransmitters and can lead to altered states of creativity and high performance. However, there is such a thing as too much feel-good hormone or dopamine. Porn, like drugs and alcohol, causes a big rush of pleasure initially, but increases tolerances, making you want more and more every time and turning you into an addict. Porn, or masturbation, also does not take you to altered states.

Law 19: Early to rise doesn't necessarily make you wise

More than a third of Asprey's guests named good sleep as critical for performance, making it the fifth most commonly cited factor. The healthiest people require less sleep, in general. Plus, when you get good-quality sleep, you need less of it.

Different bodies have different genetically predetermined circadian rhythms. Sleeping according to those instead of the way you are expected to by society or logistics can make your life much better. According to Dr. Michael Breus, well-known sleep expert, there are four chronotypes:

- **Bears** – Most common chronotype (50% of the population). Sleep-patterns follow the sun. Ready for intense tasks mid-morning. Steady energy through the day, except for a slight dip in the afternoon after lunch.

- **Lions** – Classic early birds (15% of the population). Rise before the sun is up. Because of action-packed mornings, fizzle out by evening. Turn in early.

- **Wolves** – Night owls (15% of the population). Late start to the day. Two peak periods: noon to 2 p.m. and later when the world is clocking out. Tend to be creators, introverts.

- **Dolphins** – Insomnia patients with irregular sleep routines. Light sleepers; struggle to fall asleep once they get up at night. Best work from midmorning to early afternoon.

One variable that can make it difficult for you to stick to your rhythm is light. Keep your bedroom completely dark when you go to sleep. Avoid blue light from screens just before going to sleep. Red ambient light helps with deeper sleep.

Being exposed to adequate sunlight during the day is important. It produces serotonin, which is broken down into melatonin, which helps you sleep.

Law 20: With sleep, quality matters more than duration

Sleep disorders, even minor ones like apnea, can affect your performance through the day and increase the risk of high blood pressure, diabetes, and decreased cognitive capacities. Use a sleep monitoring device to examine your sleep quality. New devices, hard mattresses, certain sleeping postures, and techniques like jaw alignment all can help improve sleep quality.

Law 21: Sleep isn't optional

Like Arianna Huffington, the founder of *Huffington Post*, many game changers come to realize the importance of rest the hard way. She believes she is accomplishing more now because she gets between seven and nine hours of sleep each night and makes time to meditate, take walks, and do yoga each day. You can focus on the length or the quality, but ensure you don't push yourself to the brink.

Law 22: Change the way you think about running

People focus so much on exercise that they forget about functional movement, wasting time and effort and becoming susceptible to injuries and reduction in sleep quality and libido. This chapter focuses on the importance of movement and exercising for game-changing results.

80 percent of people who run at least three times a week are injured within a year because they don't have motor control and the range of motion needed to run safely. Before you begin an exercise practice, master a movement practice. Work on improving posture and core strength and building muscle tissue length. Yoga helps if you want to work on your flexibility.

The number one problem is sitting too much. Intense short bursts of exercise are followed by sitting at office desks for hours.

Law 23: High performers exercise efficiently

Efficient exercise means stimulating the right hormones using the right protocols at the right times. Though there are some benefits of aerobic exercise, especially for people with high blood pressure or who are obese or sedentary or have significant visceral belly fat, long-term aerobic training has substantial negative effects like raising the cortisol (stress hormone) level. Your body also produces harmful free radicals in response to the oxygen-rich environment generated by increased respiration during aerobic exercises.

Some form of strength training is better for the long term. A combination of low- to moderate-level movement and weight training rebuilds lost muscle mass, decreases body fat, and lowers blood pressure.

Law 24: Flexibility is important to be fit

Mark Divine, a former Navy SEAL and one of Asprey's guests, relies on yoga for mental clarity and flexibility. It forms a perfect complement to the fitness program that SEALs have to undergo. The primary benefit of combining yoga with other workouts is improved spinal health, which keeps his nervous system healthier. Another benefit is detoxification of organs, allowing for greater focus. The third benefit is muscular and joint articulation flexibility.

Law 25: Eat only when you are hungry for food

The most critical aspect of performance for 75 percent of high performers interviewed by Asprey is food.

People often end up eating when they feel empty, unsafe, or unloved. Find out if your hunger is for something deeper and work to remove whatever makes you feel empty. Celebrating over a favorite meal is good as long as it doesn't turn into excessive emotional eating. Telltale signs of emotional eating include:

- Going back for seconds even if you aren't hungry
- Eating becoming a solution to cure boredom
- Relying on comfort food to feel safe, get over disappointments, relieve stress
- Failing to remember what you ate after you are done with a meal

Law 26: Eat the way your grandmother asked you to

Your ancestors had accumulated generations' worth of dietary knowledge, which cheap fast-food and homogeneity has made you gradually forget.

The genetic perspective of health says that when you fall ill you have to examine not only what you ate yesterday or last week but what your food and lifestyle choices over years and decades as well as the choices of your parents and grandparents.

The four particularly cutting-edge food-related things your grandmother must have taught you are:

· Eat small meals infrequently throughout the day. It's healthy to go for extended periods of time without eating as it makes your body dip into its fat storage for energy.

· Eat adequate proteins, particularly those rich in leucine, like dairy, beef, poultry, seafood, nuts, and seeds.

· Don't leave the table until you have eaten all your vegetables. Vegetables contain polyphenols that activate antioxidant genes in the body. Many adults might have to opt for polyphenol supplements.

· Take your daily tablespoonful of cod liver oil.

The modern diet consists of a high amount of vegetable oil or trans fats, a major source of harmful omega-6, which causes inflammatory diseases like obesity, diabetes, cancer, and Alzheimer's. Your body needs saturated fats (butter, ghee, lard, coconut oil).

Law 27: Treat the bacteria in your stomach well

The microbiome in your gut has an important symbiotic relationship with your body. Greater biodiversity in your stomach is related to cardiovascular fitness, better digestion, healthy skin, sharper brain activity, and many other benefits. Antibiotics, artificial sugars, factory-bred animals, grain-fed meat, and genetically modified foods are threatening these microscopic creatures. Prebiotic fiber, found in onions, garlic, leeks, asparagus, Jerusalem artichokes, etc., and fermented foods like yogurt and kimchi help keep the bacteria healthy.

Law 28: Use supplements to overcome the decline in your environment

The shortening of telomeres (protective end caps on your DNA) is responsible for aging. Bill Andrews, one of the world's top experts on antiaging, has found that the telomerase gene, which maintains the telomeres, can be switched on and off using different chemicals. Supplements like these are likely to become affordable in the coming years.

Among those that are more easily available now, Asprey recommends vitamin K2 (which keeps calcium in its place in the body and boosts bone and dental health), vitamin D3, vitamin A, magnesium, krill oil/ omega-3, copper, zinc, iodine, tyrosine, and methyl vitamin B12 with methyl folate.

Law 29: Make use of technology to understand your body

Self-experimentation or biohacking has been recommended by more than 450 game changers. This is done in three stages: first, you have to quantify what is going on in your body; second, you have to determine what changes need to be made; and third, you have to implement those changes.

There are many machines available now to track your body's performance, but you can also rely on feelings as the preliminary onboard sensors of your body.

Increased access to medical research and data is making more people figure out solutions on their own instead of relying on doctors; the world is moving toward an "undoctored" future.

One of the simplest diagnostics is to take your temperature every morning, which can help identify thyroid issues. Tracking aspects like sleep states, heart rate, heart rate variability and breathing rates also helps you plan your activities better. Conversely, if you are making changes to your diet or activity levels, these metrics can tell you how your body is taking it.

Companies like Viome are using such information to predict symptoms, making illnesses optional.

Law 30: Ruthlessly remove useless stressors

Your body can handle only so much stress at a time. Knowing when to push yourself hard is as important as knowing when not to push yourself hard, and knowing how to relax and recover is as important as maintaining good form when you're lifting weights.

Law 31: The greatest investment is in your health

Instead of ignoring chronic pain, use technology to cure the source of the pain. Asprey finds stem cells more useful than many other methods in this regard. Stem cell therapy has already become much cheaper than it used to be just a few years back. Stem cells are used now for recovery from injuries, slowing down aging, strengthening joints, and curing the effects of trauma.

PART 3: HAPPIER

Not one of the game changers interviewed by Asprey mentioned money as being among their top three priorities.

"When you master your base instincts and find lasting happiness, you free up huge amounts of energy that you can use to become more successful and wealthy." (Asprey, Dave, Kindle Locations 3629-3630).

Law 32: Focus your energy on doing things that matter

Genpo Roshi, a renowned Zen priest, teaches that there is a sustainable state of happiness that is not predicated on conditions, but is your basic foundation. Conditional happiness is a sign of scarcity mind-set, where you are focused on what you don't have. When you attain your material goal, you realize it doesn't make you all that happy.

Once your basic needs are met (Princeton research has found the US baseline income for this to be about $75,000), happiness from money plateaus. Once you have a modest nest egg, never put it at risk (difficult for entrepreneurs) and focus on amassing joy. Leverage your nonfinancial assets, like time, energy, creativity, instead.

Law 33: Happiness leads to wealth

Being happy unlocks a new level of potential, which makes it easier to be more productive and change your circumstances. Retail stores that score high on employee happiness levels do much higher sales than others.

Vishen Lakhiani, the founder of Mindvalley, talks about "Blisscipline," a daily methodology to hack happiness levels, which involves changing your means goals (get a degree, get a job, get married, earn a million dollars) into end goals (things you want to experience, ways in which you want to grow as a human being, and ways in which you want to contribute to the world).

Law 34: Make room in your life for things of true value

Society equates success with accumulation, but many successful people are opting for minimalism in order to find peace and meaning. Start with the simple goal of getting rid of one item that doesn't augment your life experience every day for thirty days. Look for meaning in life; align short-term actions to long-term values—happiness will follow.

Law 35: Seek out a strong community that inspires you

Being a part of a community is the second most popular piece of advice. High-quality relationships are a fundamental element of a high quality of life.

The right kind of human connection makes your brain stronger; it releases oxytocin, which makes you more generous and empathetic and reduces stress. Face-to-face communication stimulates the greatest oxytocin release; texting and social posting the least.

Law 36: You are the average of the people you spend time with

JJ Virgin attributes her son's recovery to the connections she had made through her life. Doctors volunteered to help. Strangers turned up to pray by her son's bed side.

Happiness is contagious, creating a feedback loop of relationships and more happiness if you surround yourself with happy people. Being in a community also creates a sense of safety, which calms your primitive brain. Most of all, getting involved in a community brings meaning and fulfillment to life.

Instead of seeking like-minded people all the time, seek like-hearted people who challenge you and help you grow. Meeting people with different opinions will help you accept conflict and become peaceful.

Law 37: Invest in intimate relationships

People in relationships are, on average, happier. Marriage isn't the only type of relationship that offers happiness— young people are embracing polyamory and other nontraditional types of relationships that might not meet society's approval but make them happy.

Relationships work better with the support of the community. And communities might come to accept frowned upon forms of companionship like polyamory, which provides stability and security along with self-actualization for the partners.

Once you are in a relationship, work as hard at it as you would in the gym or on your career.

Law 38: Learn to control the voice in your head

Meditation is one of the top pieces of advice from many game changers. A sustained practice of any form of meditation makes you more aware of your automatic thoughts and impulses, helping you control them better.

Meditation helps lessen your body's chemical response to stress by enhancing the workings of the parasympathetic nervous system, which is the source of rest and relaxation. It also strengthens the brain's prefrontal cortex.

Begin meditating by letting go of expectations, letting things happen, and accepting whatever thoughts come up. Observe your thoughts; understand how they get triggered automatically by external stimuli. This teaches you to consciously choose to react with anger or fear or to not react at all. With repetition and time, new neural pathways will develop that favor being happy, calm, peaceful, focused, and creative as opposed to reactive, angry, and resistant. What meditation or mindfulness allows anyone to do is to draw the line between useful and constructive anguish and useless rumination.

Law 39: Use your breath to your benefit

Wim Hof, who holds Guinness World Records for withstanding extreme temperatures, teaches breathing techniques that can cleanse tissues from inside and create more cellular energy. The three steps involve deep breathing, gradual exposure to cold, and mind-set. Warm up by inhaling deeply, holding for a moment, exhaling, and holding the exhalation for as long as you can. After repeating this fifteen times, inhale through your nose and exhale through your mouth in short powerful bursts about thirty times.

Other guests have learned techniques from meditation teachers in India that thicken the strip that connects the right and left sides of the brain, and provide energy or relaxation depending on the speed with which you perform them.

Law 40: Learn to meditate faster for better return on your time investment

Learn meditation from genuine teachers using high-quality techniques to ensure you are doing it right. Use methods like heart rate variability training to learn how to get into meditative states more easily. Sound and light can be used to enhance meditation. Asprey has even tried EEG to train people in meditation.

Law 41: Get out of your domesticated environment into the wild

Spending time in nature nourishes you brain and gut, helps cells create more energy, lessens the effects of depression, and lets you perform better when indoors.

Look at your lifestyle and ask yourself how you can reinstate some of the things that are natural to the human species, things that make indigenous people in many pockets of the world healthier, stronger, and fitter. Humans have been living like farm animals—brainwashed for maximum productivity. To keep your genetic code from degenerating, you need to create a zoo, a habitat and diet that are as similar to the wild as possible. This doesn't mean living off the grid, but reducing toxic load and improving the quality of your diet and exposure to fresh air, sunlight, soil, and clean water.

Law 42: Don't shun sunlight

Sunlight helps create EZ water and vitamin D in the body and adds electrons to your cells, supports the circadian rhythm, and has many other benefits. Seasonal depression is caused by low exposure to sunlight. The fear of sunburn or skin cancer makes people slather on sunscreen, use sunglasses, and cover themselves up, when the body thrives in natural sunlight. The gut bacteria aid in the production of melanin, which naturally protects the body from sunlight, but food habits are destroying the microbiome inside humans.

If exposure to sunlight is impossible, try to find an indoor full-spectrum light that emits at least 2,500 without using LED lights. Start at just five or ten minutes of exposure a day, depending on your light's power, and work your way up to no more than sixty minutes.

Law 44: Get dirty

Exposing yourself to bacteria is transformative for the whole body, from the development of the gut to the development of the immune system to healthy brain function. Studies are being conducted to prove possible beneficial effects of soil bacteria on depression and PTSD. Take a nature-walk or a forest bath, or spend time in a park to reduce stress, boost immunity, and increase longevity. Encourage kids to get dirty.

Law 44: Use gratitude to turn off fear

"If you were to skip every other chapter in this book and read just this one, you'd still be ahead of the game. Gratitude is that important." (Asprey, Dave, Kindle Locations 4644–4645).

According to the Polyvagal Theory, the vagus nerve starts at your brain stem, wanders through the body, and monitors information to report it back to the brain. The strength of its activity is known as your vagal tone. If you have a high vagal tone, you can relax more quickly after a stressful episode; a low vagal tone keeps you chronically agitated. Social interaction and care-giving help enhance the vagal tone, as does feeling gratitude.

When you are in a state of gratitude, your nervous system is getting cues of safety. Safety cues like listening to or conversing in soothing voices or imagining being in a happy place help you calm down after stressful episodes. Before going to bed in the evening, if you think of something that you are grateful for, you wake up in a better mood and not anticipating stress. Do not put yourself into a stressed state by anticipating problems before they occur.

Law 45: Gratitude is the doorway to forgiveness

Forgiveness reprograms your nervous system to stop reacting to memories of suffering. To forgive, identify the false stories you tell yourself and find a way to be grateful for the worst of things. Don't be sorry; just forgive.

Forgiveness is often a matter of reframing. People have enough to be grateful for, but they choose to indulge in self-pity. Gratitude takes you out of your story of self-pity. Forgiveness lets you stop carrying other people's grudges, but it has to accompany gratitude to mean anything. Once you feel gratitude and offer forgiveness, you will be freer to attempt things you have been telling yourself are impossible.

Law 46: Exercise the gratitude muscle

You can foster habits to experience gratitude cognitively and physiologically.

· Spend five minutes every day to note down the good things that have happened to you that day. Visualize them in great sensory detail. Ask yourself about that one thing you could have done to make the day better.

· Practice mindfulness. Relax and appreciate the beauty around you. Take a gratitude walk.

· Rethink a negative situation. Feel your negative emotions, but find positives in any situation, too.

· Actively look for things that you authentically appreciate.

· Practice gratitude with loved ones. Ask your children to relate acts of kindness at the dinner table to get them to sleep calmly.

- Write a thank-you note to someone who has touched your life in a meaningful way.

- Practice combining gratitude and forgiveness. Note down something that has hurt you, feel the negative emotion, then think of a way the situation has shaped who you are, and let go of the negativity.

EDITORIAL REVIEW

In *Game Changers: What Leaders, Innovators, and Mavericks Do to Win at Life*, Dave Asprey shares the pointers he has collected from over 400 top performers across many fields while interviewing them for his extremely popular podcast *Bulletproof Radio*. As the author states in his introduction to this impressive feat of data crunching, the intent was not to know what these outliers achieved or how they achieved it, but to discover the most important things that powered their achievements.

What emerges is a collection of 46 laws, neatly divided across three categories targeted to affect the brain, the body, and overall happiness. Some of these laws would be well-known to any reader of self-help books or, indeed, anyone with common sense (learn to say "no," never give in to fear, look for meaning and not money, meditate), while others might surprise, or even vex, people unfamiliar with Asprey's podcast. The latter category includes hacks of questionable merit like microdosing on LSD and other "smart drugs" and restricting ejaculation for men to balance hormones.

Asprey is no stranger to controversial claims, of course, with his earlier treatise on the Bulletproof diet having been called a "caricature of a bad fad-diet book." He does qualify most of the less mainstream recommendations in the book by adding that techniques that worked for him may not work for others. These laws are no commandments to be followed to the letter, but a road map to be used to set one's own priorities, a menu of options that the reader can choose from. The relative independence of each law also helps in that one can select those that seem appealing to begin with and set off on the path to becoming a game changer and "kicking ass."

What does deserve merit is the underlying theme of the book—looking beyond the traditional definitions of success (money, power, and attractiveness) at factors like forgiveness, gratitude, self-awareness, purpose, and passion that make life truly meaningful. Techniques like meditation and controlled breathing that have been popular in many cultures for centuries deserve as many spokespeople as they can get. The book also takes well-deserved potshots at some of Western culture's obsessions like fast food, antibiotics, rising early, and stringent standards of hygiene that have led to ill-health, dissatisfaction, and depression.

There is, then, enough in the book that would prove worthwhile even for the skeptic, tired of impractical self-help tomes. The wide range of interviewees, even if there seems to be a bias towards other biohackers of his ilk, adds extra credibility to the many suggestions strewn through these chapters. If someone's genuinely interested in taking the first steps towards changing their habits for the better, they could do much worse than to pick up this largely sensible and quick-paced volume.

BACKGROUND ON AUTHOR

Dave Asprey (b. October 30, 1973) is an American entrepreneur and Silicon Valley investor. He earned his undergraduate degree in computer information systems from California State University and an MBA from the Wharton School. After working in companies like Bradshaw, 3Com, Exodus Communications, Citrix Systems, and Trend Micro, Asprey founded Bulletproof 360, Inc. in 2013 and Bulletproof Nutrition Inc. in 2014. Apart from having been a *New York Times* bestselling author, he has written for the *New York Times* and *Fortune*.

He is also a professional biohacker, the creator of Bulletproof Coffee, and the host of the Webby Award-winning podcast *Bulletproof Radio*. The stated goal of the Bulletproof brand is to enhance human performance. Despite the popularity of the brand, his Bulletproof diet has also been widely criticized for being unscientific. Asprey does not have any medical or nutritional training.

He has stated that he aims to live to the age of 180 and has spent millions of dollars hacking his own biology through stem cells injections, about 100 daily supplements, infrared light bathing, and using a hyperbaric oxygen chamber. He met his wife, a physician, at an anti-aging conference.

OTHER TITLES BY DAVE ASPREY

The Better Baby Book (2013) (co-authored with his wife Dr. Lana Asprey)

The Bulletproof Diet (2014)

Bulletproof: The Cookbook (2015)

Head Strong (2017)

END OF BOOK SUMMARY

Made in the USA
Las Vegas, NV
08 March 2022

45243526R00026